Published by Polshek Partnership, LLP
320 West 13th Street
New York, NY 10014

Books in this series
  Brooklyn Museum Entry Pavilion and Plaza
  Sarah Lawrence College, Heimbold Visual Arts Center
  William J. Clinton Presidential Center and Park
  New York Hall of Science
  Scandinavia House
  Holland Performing Arts Center
  Mercersburg Academy Burgin Center
  Lycée Français de New York

ISBN 0-9772502-1-0
Library of Congress Control Number: 2005908357

9908   WILLIAM J. CLINTON PRESIDENTIAL
       CENTER AND PARK

This is one in a series of books, each of which
tells the story of a single building. It is our hope
that as these little books accumulate alongside
our body of work, they, in their aggregate, will
form a profile of our design intentions.

Polshek Partnership Architects

This library tells the story of America at the end of the 20th century, of a dramatically different time in the way we worked and lived. We moved out of the Cold War into an age of interdependence with new possibilities and new dangers. We moved out of an industrial economy into an information-age economy. We moved out of a period when we were obsessed with overcoming the legacy of slavery and discrimination against African-Americans to a point where we were challenged to deal with an explosion of diversity, of people from all races and ethnic groups and religions from around the world, and we had to change the role of government to deal with that.

President William J. Clinton
from remarks at the dedication of the
Presidential Center and Park
November 18, 2004

a

b

north/south grid

little rock grid

GEOGRAPHY

Little Rock lies at the confluence of Arkansas's major physiographic regions: the folded mountain terrain of the Ouachitas and Ozarks to the west and north, the great Delta of the Arkansas and Mississippi Rivers to the east and the Timberlands to the south. This juncture is apparent in Little Rock itself, with hills visible to the west along the Arkansas River and oxbow lakes along the flatter, broader floodplain to the east.

Two major street grid systems intersect the site. A north-south grid extends across the River and forms the major organizational framework for both North Little Rock and the southern and eastern sectors of Little Rock; the Rock Island Railroad Bridge and the I-30 Highway Bridge conform to this geometry. The second grid rotates to orient downtown Little Rock to the Arkansas River as it bends towards the west.

a   Topographic analysis: mountain ridges in the
     west and oxbow lakes in the northeast
b   Street analysis

a

b

a   Panorama of Little Rock, c.1910
Following the Civil War, a building boom in
little Rock resulted in the construction of
many commercial buildings on the
street once called East Markham Street,
now known as President Clinton Avenue

b   Arkansas Railroad Map, 1895
In the late 1800s, three railroads were
located on the north bank of the
Arkansas River

c   Perspective map of Little Rock, 1887

PERSPECTIVE MAP OF THE CITY OF

LITTLE ROCK, ARK.

STATE CAPITAL OF ARKANSAS.

COUNTY SEAT OF PULASKI COUNTY

c

a

b

a   Panorama looking west with site in
    foreground, ca. 1999
b   Choctaw Passenger Station, 1988
c   Rock Island Railroad Bridge, 1994

c

The Site

City Grids

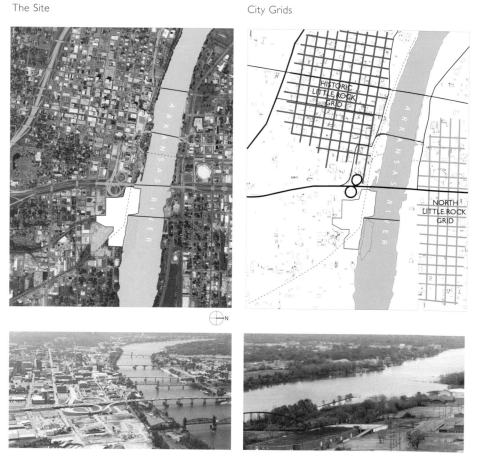

ARKANSAS RIVER

HISTORIC LITTLE ROCK GRID

ARKANSAS RIVER

NORTH LITTLE ROCK GRID

view to the west

view to the east

Land Use

Green Space

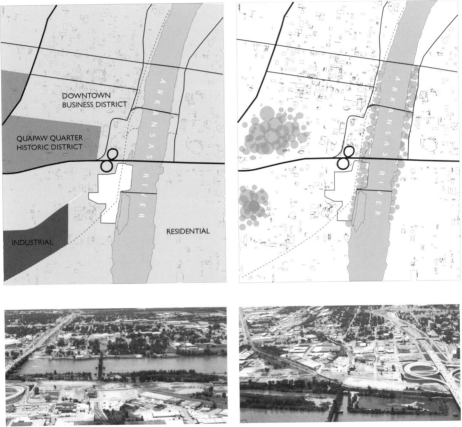

DOWNTOWN
BUSINESS DISTRICT

ARKANSAS RIVER

QUAPAW QUARTER
HISTORIC DISTRICT

RESIDENTIAL

INDUSTRIAL

ARKANSAS RIVER

view to the north

view to the south

THREE EARLY SCHEMES

Precedents

Villa Rotunda

Campidoglio

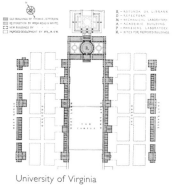

University of Virginia

The Villa

The Piazza

The Campus

Chateau de Chenonceau

BUILDING AS BRIDGE
The earliest schemes placed the building parallel to the River and ended up covering a great deal of land. Once we turned the building perpendicular to the River and elevated it like a bridge fragment, the site was preserved, and allowed the park to run continuously underneath, emphasizing the public nature of the site.

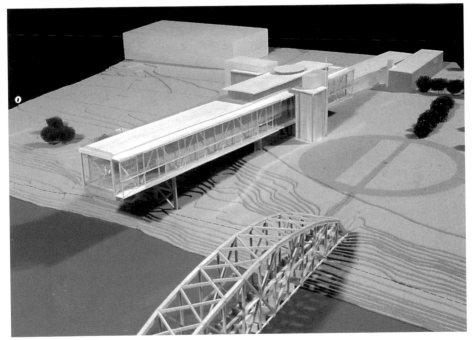

a

THE SEVENTH BRIDGE

Together with Hargreaves Associates we
identified two primary site design objectives:
first, to recognize the iconic significance of the
six bridges that cross the Arkanas River; and
second, to enhance Little Rock's park system.
With the recognition that the best view from
the site was to the west, with the six bridges as
the defining element, the idea of the building as
connecting bridge became central. The
President immediately drew a connection
between the proposed scheme and his "Bridge
to the 21st Century", the metaphor for his
Administration's achievements. Moreover, the
new building is cast as mediator between the
past, represented by the Rock Island Railroad
Bridge, which will be restored as a pedestrian
connection with North Little Rock, and the
Choctaw Station, which houses the Clinton
Foundation and School of Public Service, the
future.

a   Little Rock's six bridges
b   The Bridge Scheme

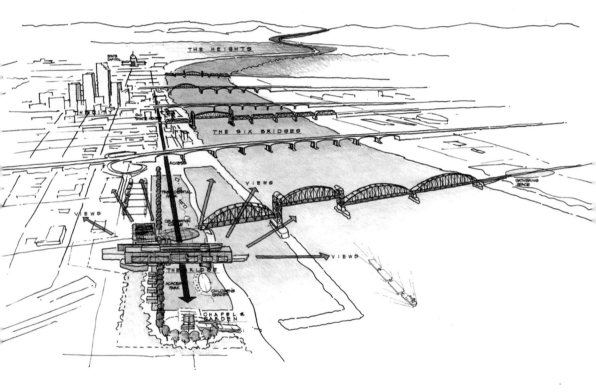

b

21

Fall/Winter 1999
Sketches of bridge scheme alternates and
relationship to the Rock Island Bridge and
President Clinton Avenue

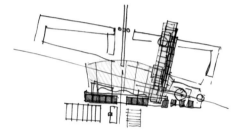

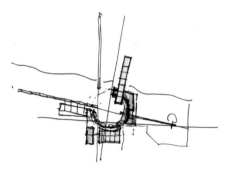

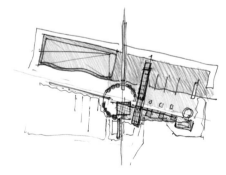

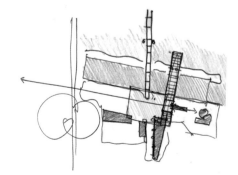

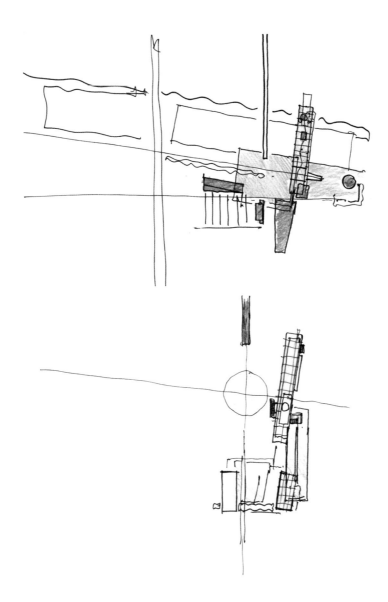

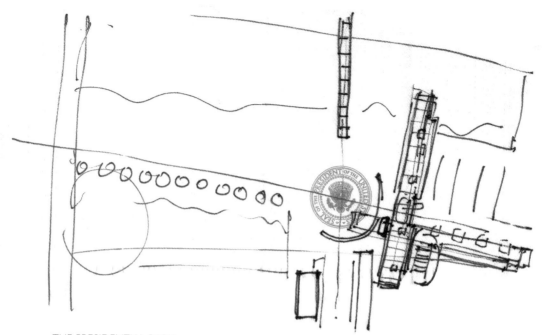

THE PRESIDENTIAL PARK

The organizational framework of the site is generated by the extension of President Clinton Avenue to create an upland pedestrian promenade from downtown to the front door of the Center, and by the extension of the axis of the Rock Island Railroad Bridge to the south to reconnect the Bridge to its historic rail station.

The intersection of these two axes is marked by the primary arrival and celebratory plaza—the Celebration Circle—around which are sited the major building components of the complex and the major open spaces. These spaces are organized by a series of secondary pathways also laid out on the geometries of the President Clinton Avenue (downtown Little Rock) and Rock Island Railroad Bridge (north-south) grids.

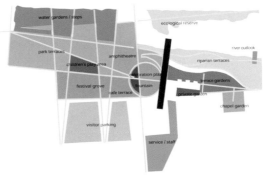

a

b

26

a   Fourteen-foot-long schematic design
     phase model
b   Model detail, Celebration Circle
c   Section sketch: mechanical
     services are located in a dedicated
     floor, allowing Museum floors to be
     unencumbered
d   Schematic design meeting with President
     Clinton

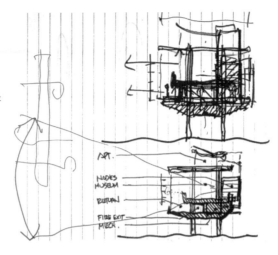

c

d

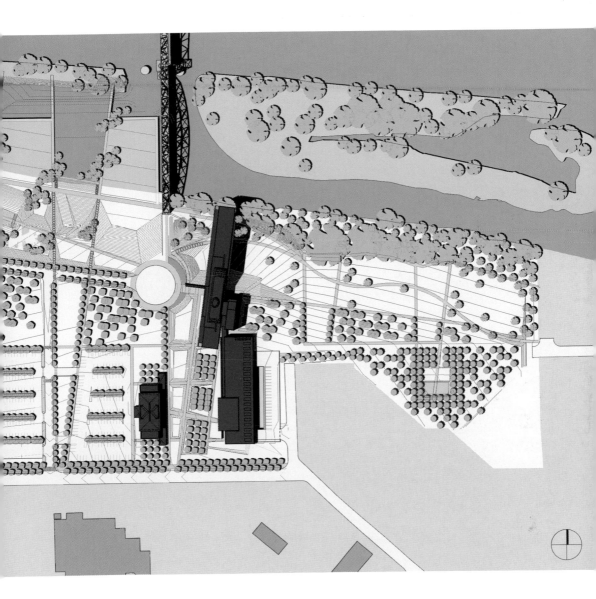

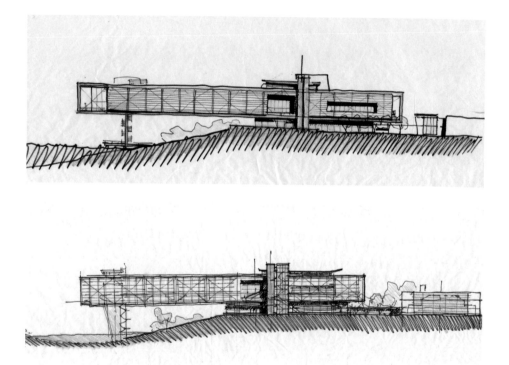

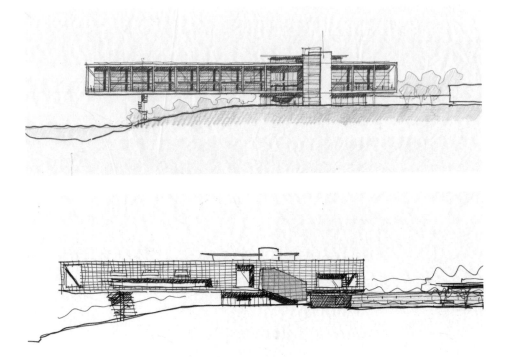

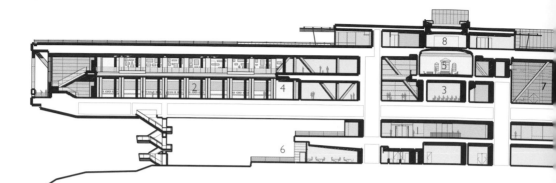

The organization of the Museum exhibits was inspired by the interior of the Long Room in the Old Library in Trinity College Dublin, designed between 1712 and 1732 by Thomas Burgh

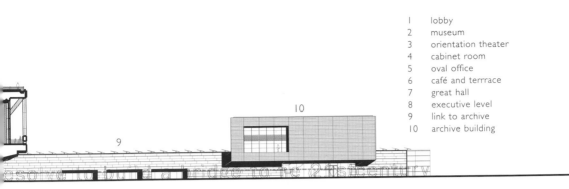

1   lobby
2   museum
3   orientation theater
4   cabinet room
5   oval office
6   café and terrrace
7   great hall
8   executive level
9   link to archive
10   archive building

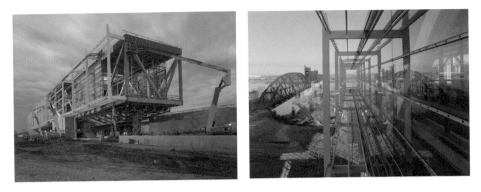

INTRODUCTION TO THREE SPEECHES
An Architecture of Democracy

How does one define an architecture of democracy, or interpret such an abstract idea or value in built form?

From the very beginning, President Clinton's mandate to us was that his presidential library be open, inviting, grand, accessible and democratic. Ancient and modern precedents are legion, sharing clear geometry, platonic form, rational thought and clarity of expression. Countless buildings invoke the classical language of Greece and Rome – porticoes, pediments, domes and colonnades – to express the public identities and democratic ideals of cultural, educational and governmental institutions; modern examples such as Chandigarh, Dacca, and Brasilia employ forms that bespeak the monumentality and gravity of the idea of democracy. All testify to the associative power of architecture. But what of the inherent tension between monumentality and intellectual and physical accessibility?

Our design explorations led to a crystalline bridge, whose formal and material qualities sponsor multiple readings that, taken together, aspire to resolve this tension. In form and structure, the design resonates with the landscape and riverscape of Little Rock, directly engaging the City's iconic "Six Bridges" and alluding to the President's aspiration to "build a bridge to the 21st century." The strength of the Administration and the President's commitment to a free and open society are expressed through the truss structure and its dramatic 90-foot-long cantilevers. The elevation of the building ensures the physical continuity of the landscape, allowing it to flow uninterrupted beneath the building. The building's transparency and luminosity speak to openness, while the material layering and the iterative unfolding of the experiential sequence speak to the depth and breadth of the President's policy initiatives.

The speeches woven through the following visual narrative are the President's: excerpts from his January 20, 1993 Inaugural Address, the January 27, 2000 State of the Union Address and the November 18, 2004 Dedication of the Presidential Center and Park. The words are optimistic, grave, discerning, compassionate, confident, thoughtful and accessible. It is our hope that our building is, in some measure, read as emblematic of the brilliance and complexity of the man and the richness of his presidency.

Richard M. Olcott and James S. Polshek
Polshek Partnership Architects
May 2006

My fellow citizens, today we celebrate the mystery of American renewal. This ceremony is held in the depth of winter, but by the words we speak and the faces we show the world, we force the spring, a spring reborn in the world's oldest democracy that brings forth the vision and courage to reinvent America. When our Founders boldly declared America's independence to the world and our purposes to the Almighty, they knew that America, to endure, would have to change; not change for change's sake but change to preserve America's ideals: life, liberty, the pursuit of happiness. Though we march to the music of our time, our mission is timeless. Each generation of Americans must define what it means to be an American.

On behalf of our Nation, I salute my predecessor, President Bush, for his half-century of service to America. And I thank the millions of men and women whose steadfastness and sacrifice triumphed over depression, fascism, and communism.

Today, a generation raised in the shadows of the cold war assumes new responsibilities in a world warmed by the sunshine of freedom but threatened still by ancient hatreds and new plagues. Raised in unrivaled prosperity, we inherit an economy that is still the world's strongest but is weakened by business failures, stagnant wages, increasing inequality, and deep divisions among our own people.

When George Washington first took the oath I have just sworn to uphold, news traveled slowly across the land by horseback and across the ocean by boat. Now, the sights and sounds of this ceremony are broadcast instantaneously to billions around the world. Communications and commerce are global. Investment is mobile. Technology is almost magical. And ambition for a better life is now universal.

We earn our livelihood in America today in peaceful competition with people all across the Earth. Profound and powerful forces are shaking and remaking our world. And the urgent question of our time is whether we can make change our friend and not our enemy. This new world has already enriched the lives of millions of Americans who are able to compete and win in it. But when most people are working harder for less; when others cannot work at all; when the cost of health care devastates families and threatens to bankrupt our enterprises, great and small; when the fear of crime robs law-abiding citizens of their freedom; and when millions of poor children cannot even imagine the lives we are calling them to lead, we have not made change our friend.

We know we have to face hard truths and take strong steps, but we have not done so; instead, we have drifted. And that drifting has eroded our resources, fractured our economy, and shaken our confidence. Though our challenges are fearsome, so are our strengths. Americans have ever been a restless, questing, hopeful people. And we must bring to our task today the vision and will of those who came before us. From our Revolution to the Civil War, to the Great Depression, to the civil rights movement, our people have always mustered the determination to construct from these crises the pillars of our history. Thomas Jefferson believed that to preserve the very foundations of our Nation, we would need dramatic change from time to time. Well, my fellow Americans, this is our time. Let us embrace it.

Our democracy must be not only the envy of the world but the engine of our own renewal. There is nothing wrong with America that cannot be cured by what is right with America. And so today we pledge an end to the era of deadlock and drift, and a new season of American renewal has begun.

To renew America, we must be bold. We must do what no generation has had to do before. We must invest more in our own people, in their jobs, and in their future, and at the same time cut our massive debt. And we must do so in a world in which we must compete for every opportunity. It will not be easy. It will require sacrifice, but it can be done and done fairly, not choosing sacrifice for its own sake but for our own sake. We must provide for our Nation the way a family provides for its children.

Our Founders saw themselves in the light of posterity. We can do no less. Anyone who has ever watched a child's eyes wander into sleep knows what posterity is. Posterity is the world to come: the world for whom we hold our ideals, from whom we have borrowed our planet, and to whom we bear sacred responsibility. We must do what America does best: offer more opportunity to all and demand more responsibility from all. It is time to break the bad habit of expecting something for nothing from our Government or from each other. Let us all take more responsibility not only for ourselves and our families but for our communities and our country.

To renew America, we must revitalize our democracy. This beautiful Capital, like every capital since the dawn of civilization, is often a place of intrigue and calculation. Powerful people maneuver for position and worry endlessly about who is in and who is out, who is up and who is down, forgetting those people whose toil and sweat sends us here and pays our way. Americans deserve better. And in this city today there are people who want to do better. And so I say to all of you here: Let us resolve to reform our politics so that power and privilege no longer shout down the voice of the people. Let us put aside personal advantage so that we can feel the pain and see the promise of America. Let us resolve to make our Government a place for what Franklin Roosevelt called bold, persistent experimentation, a Government for our tomorrows, not our yesterdays. Let us give this Capital back to the people to whom it belongs.

To renew America, we must meet challenges abroad as well as at home. There is no longer a clear division between what is foreign and what is domestic. The world economy, the world environment, the world AIDS crisis, the world arms race: they affect us all. Today, as an older order passes, the new world is more free but less stable. Communism's collapse has called forth old animosities and new dangers. Clearly, America must continue to lead the world we did so much to make.

While America rebuilds at home, we will not shrink from the challenges nor fail to seize the opportunities of this new world. Together with our friends and allies, we will work to shape change, lest it engulf us. When our vital interests are challenged or the will and conscience of the international community is defied, we will act, with peaceful diplomacy whenever possible, with force when necessary. The brave Americans serving our Nation today in the Persian Gulf, in Somalia, and wherever else they stand are testament to our resolve. But our greatest strength is the power of our ideas, which are still new in many lands. Across the world we see them embraced, and we rejoice. Our hopes, our hearts, our hands are with those on every continent who are building democracy and freedom. Their cause is America's cause.

The American people have summoned the change we celebrate today. You have raised your voices in an unmistakable chorus. You have cast your votes in historic numbers. And you have changed the face of Congress, the Presidency, and the political process itself. Yes, you, my fellow Americans, have forced the spring. Now we must do the work the season demands. To that work I now turn with all the authority of my office. I ask the Congress to join with me. But no President, no Congress, no Government can undertake this mission alone.

My fellow Americans, you, too, must play your part in our renewal. I challenge a new generation of young Americans to a season of service: to act on your idealism by helping troubled children, keeping company with those in need, reconnecting our torn communities. There is so much to be done; enough, indeed, for millions of others who are still young in spirit to give of themselves in service, too. In serving, we recognize a simple but powerful truth: We need each other, and we must care for one another.

The 1899 revitalized Choctaw Railroad Passenger Station is home to the University of Arkansas's Clinton School of Public Service, the Clinton Public Policy Institute and the William J. Clinton Foundation

Today we do more than celebrate America. We rededicate ourselves to the very idea of America, an idea born in revolution and renewed through two centuries of challenge; an idea tempered by the knowledge that, but for fate, we, the fortunate, and the unfortunate might have been each other; an idea ennobled by the faith that our Nation can summon from its myriad diversity the deepest measure of unity; an idea infused with the conviction that America's long, heroic journey must go forever upward.

And so, my fellow Americans, as we stand at the edge of the 21st century, let us begin anew with energy and hope, with faith and discipline. And let us work until our work is done. The Scripture says, "And let us not be weary in well doing: for in due season we shall reap, if we faint not." From this joyful mountaintop of celebration we hear a call to service in the valley. We have heard the trumpets. We have changed the guard. And now, each in our own way and with God's help, we must answer the call.

Thank you, and God bless you all.

The President spoke on January 20, 1993 at 12:01 p.m. at the West Front of the Capitol

While the 80-million pieces of paper and over 80,000 museum objects of the presidential archive are located in a secure, below-grade environment, the archivists occupy the light-filled glass and steel research facility above. A stainless steel perforated corrugated screen wraps the exterior curtain wall, reducing solar heat gain and glare in the office spaces

ADDRESS BEFORE A JOINT SESSION OF THE
CONGRESS ON THE STATE OF THE UNION,
JANUARY 27TH, 2000 (excerpt)

Mr. Speaker, Mr. Vice President, Members of Congress, honored guests, my fellow Americans:

We are fortunate to be alive at this moment in history. Never before has our Nation enjoyed, at once, so much prosperity and social progress with so little internal crisis and so few external threats. Never before have we had such a blessed opportunity and, therefore, such a profound obligation to build the more perfect Union of our Founders' dreams.

We begin the new century with over 20 million new jobs; the fastest economic growth in more than 30 years; the lowest unemployment rates in 30 years; the lowest poverty rates in 20 years; the lowest African-American and Hispanic unemployment rates on record; the first back-to-back surpluses in 42 years; and next month, America will achieve the longest period of economic growth in our entire history. We have built a new economy.

And our economic revolution has been matched by a revival of the American spirit: crime down by 20 percent, to its lowest level in 25 years; teen births down 7 years in a row; adoptions up by 30 percent; welfare rolls cut in half, to their lowest levels in 30 years.

My fellow Americans, the state of our Union is the strongest it has ever been.

As always, the real credit belongs to the American people. My gratitude also goes to those of you in this Chamber who have worked with us to put progress over partisanship.

Eight years ago, it was not so clear to most Americans there would be much to celebrate in the year 2000. Then our Nation was gripped by economic distress, social decline, political gridlock. The title of a best-selling book asked: "America: What Went Wrong?"

In the best traditions of our Nation, Americans determined to set things right. We restored the vital center, replacing outmoded ideologies with a new vision anchored in basic, enduring values: opportunity for all, responsibility from all, a community of all Americans. We reinvented Government, transforming it into a catalyst for new ideas that stress both opportunity and responsibility and give our people the tools they need to solve their own problems.

With the smallest Federal work force in 40 years, we turned record deficits into record surpluses and doubled our investment in education. We cut crime with 100,000 community police and the Brady law, which has kept guns out of the hands of half a million criminals.

We ended welfare as we knew it, requiring work while protecting health care and nutrition for children and investing more in child care, transportation, and housing to help their parents go to work. We've helped parents to succeed at home and at work with family leave, which 20 million Americans have now used to care for a newborn child or a sick loved one. We've engaged 150,000 young Americans in citizen service through AmeriCorps, while helping them earn money for college.

In 1992, we just had a roadmap. Today, we have results.

Even more important, America again has the confidence to dream big dreams. But we must not let this confidence drift into complacency. For we, all of us, will be judged by the dreams and deeds we pass on to our children. And on that score, we will be held to a high standard, indeed, because our chance to do good is so great.

My fellow Americans, we have crossed the bridge we built to the 21st century. Now, we must shape a 21st century American revolution of opportunity, responsibility, and community. We must be now, as we were in the beginning, a new nation.

At the dawn of the last century, Theodore Roosevelt said, "The one characteristic more essential than any other is foresight . . . it should be the growing Nation with a future that takes the long look ahead." So tonight let us take our long look ahead and set great goals for our Nation.

To 21st century America, let us pledge these things: Every child will begin school ready to learn and graduate ready to succeed. Every family will be able to succeed at home and at work, and no child will be raised in poverty. We will meet the challenge of the aging of America. We will assure quality, affordable health care, at last, for all Americans. We will make America the safest big country on Earth. We will pay off our national debt for the first time since 1835. We will bring prosperity to every American community. We will reverse the course of climate change and leave a safer, cleaner planet. America will lead the world toward shared peace and prosperity and the far frontiers of science and technology. And we will become at last what our Founders pledged us to be so long ago: One Nation, under God, indivisible, with liberty and justice for all.

These are great goals, worthy of a great nation. We will not reach them all this year, not even in this decade. But we will reach them. Let us remember that the first American Revolution was not won with a single shot; the continent was not settled in a single year. The lesson of our history and the lesson of the last 7 years is that great goals are reached step by step, always building on our progress, always gaining ground. Of course, you can't gain ground if you're standing still. And for too long this Congress has been standing still on some of our most pressing national priorities. So let's begin tonight with them.

The President spoke on January 27, 2000 at 9:18 p.m. in the House Chamber of the Capitol

REMARKS AT THE DEDICATION OF THE WILLIAM J. CLINTON PRESIDENTIAL LIBRARY AND PARK, NOVEMBER 18, 2004 (excerpt)

This library tells the story of America at the end of the 20th century, of a dramatically different time in the way we worked and lived. We moved out of the Cold War into an age of interdependence with new possibilities and new dangers. We moved out of an information — I mean, an industrial economy into an information-age economy. We moved out of a period when we were obsessed with overcoming the legacy of slavery and discrimination against African- Americans to a point where we were challenged to deal with an explosion of diversity, of people from all races and ethnic groups and religions from around the world, and we had to change the role of government to deal with that.

That whole story is here, in 80 million documents, 21 million e-mails — two of them mine — (laughter) — 2 million photographs, and 80,000 artifacts. In the interests of openness and public access, we are asking more than 100,000 of these documents to be opened early before the law requires.

I thank those who are working on the Clinton School of Public Service, because I want more young people to go into public service.
I thank those who are working in Harlem and here on my foundation or who visit us on the Internet, as Hillary said, at clintonfoundation.org,

who help us to promote religious and racial reconciliation, to advance citizen service, to promote economic empowerment for poor people in poor communities, and to continue the fight against AIDS. In three years in Africa, the Caribbean, India and China, we have succeeded in cutting the price of the testing equipment and generic drugs by 70 percent, and we hope by 2006, and expect, to serve over 2 million people with medicine who were not getting it on the day I left office.

Now this library, of course, is primarily about my presidency. I want to say a special word of thanks to Al Gore and to Tipper for the indispensable contribution that they made. And I told Al today that this library won an international environmental award, even though it's got a lot of glass. Because of solar panels and a lot of other improvements, we cut the energy usage here by 34 percent. So Al, thanks for the inspiration, and I'm still trying to measure up to the challenge you set for me so long ago.

I believe the job of a president is to understand and explain the time in which he serves, to set forth a vision of where we need to go and a strategy of how to get there, and then to pursue it with all his mind and heart — bending only in the face of error or new circumstances and the crises which are unforeseen, a problem that affects all of us.

When I became president the world was a new and very different place, as I said. And I thought about how we ought to confront it. America has two great dominant strands of political thought; we're represented up here on this stage: conservatism, which at its very best draws lines that should not be crossed; and progressivism,

which at its very best breaks down barriers that are no longer needed or should never have been erected in the first place.

It seemed to me that in 1992 we needed to do both to prepare America for the 21st century — to be more conservative in things like erasing the deficit and paying down the debt, and preventing crime and punishing criminals, and protecting and supporting families, and enforcing things like child support laws, and reforming the military to meet the new challenges of the 21st century. And we needed to be more progressive in creating good jobs, reducing poverty, increasing the quality of public education, opening the doors of college to all, increasing access to health care, investing more in science and technology, and building new alliances with our former adversaries, and working for peace across the world and peace in America, across all the lines that divide us.

Now when I proposed to do both, we said that all of them were consistent with the great American values of opportunity, responsibility and community. We labeled the approach "New Democrat." It then became known as "the Third Way." It was — as it was embraced by progressive parties across the world. But I like the slogan we had way back in 1992, "putting people first," because in the end, I always kept score by a simple measure: Were ordinary people better off when I stopped than when I started?

I grew up in the pre-television age, in a family of uneducated but smart, hard-working, caring storytellers. They taught me that everyone has a story. And that made politics intensely personal to me. It was about giving people better stories.

That's why I asked those six people to talk here today. When I think of the Family Leave Law, I think of that good man who brought his dying daughter to see me in the White House on a Sunday morning, and who grabbed me as I walked away and said, "The time I got to take off from work was the most important time in my life."

I think of people like that fine woman who worked herself out of welfare and now runs her own business. I remember the first woman I ever talked to who went from welfare to work. I said, "What's the best thing about it?" She said, "When my boy goes to school and they say, 'What does your mama do for a living,' he can give an answer." Those are the things that make politics real to me, at home and around the world.

The record is all in there — what we did at

home, what we did abroad. I thank Bono for singing about Northern Ireland and President Bush for mentioning the Balkans. There were many other places we tried to help.

But the record is there. Even where we fell short, we pushed forward. And what I want to say is, if you think of the biggest disappointment around the world to me, I tried so hard for peace in the Middle East. I thank Shimon Peres and the children of Yitzhak Rabin and Ehud Barak for being here today, and the current foreign minister of Israel for being here today. I did all I could.

But when we had seven years of progress toward peace, there was one whole year when, for the first time in the history of the state of Israel, not one person died of a terrorist attack, when the Palestinians began to believe they could have a shared future. And so, Mr. President, again, I say: I hope you get to cross over into the promised land of Middle East peace. We have a good opportunity, and we are all praying for you.

(Applause)

Finally, let me say this. Quite apart from all the details, the thing I want most is for people who come to this library, whether they're Republicans or Democrats, liberals or conservatives, to see that public service is noble and important, that the choices and decisions leaders make affect the lives of millions of Americans and people all across the world.

I want young people to want to see not only what I did with my life, but to see what they could do with their lives. Because this is mostly

the story of what we, the people, can do when we work together.

Yes, this library is the symbol of a bridge, a bridge to the 21st century. It's been called one of the great achievements of the new age, and a British magazine said it looked like a glorified house trailer. And I thought, well, that's about me, you know? I'm a little red and a little blue.

(Laughter)

What it is to me is the symbol of not only what I tried to do but what I want to do with the rest of my life — building bridges from yesterday to tomorrow, building bridges across racial and religious and ethnic and income and political divides.

Building bridges.

I believe our mission in this new century is clear. For good or ill, we live in an interdependent world. We can't escape each other. And while we have to fight our enemies, we can't possibly kill, jail or occupy all of them. Therefore, we have to spend our lives building a global community and an American community of shared responsibilities, shared values, shared benefits. What are those values? And I want to say this. This is important. I don't want to be too political here, but it bothers me when America gets as divided as it was. I once said to a friend of mine, about three days before the election — I heard all these terrible things — I said, "You know, am I the only person in the entire United States of America who likes both George W. Bush and John Kerry, who believes they're both good people, who believes they both love our country and they just see the world differently?"

What should our shared values be? Everybody counts. Everybody deserves a chance. Everybody's got a responsibility to fulfill. We all do better when we work together. Our differences do matter, but our common humanity matters more.

So I tell you we can continue building our bridge to tomorrow. It will require some red American line-drawing and some blue American barrier-breaking, but we can do it together.

Thank you and God bless you.

(Applause)

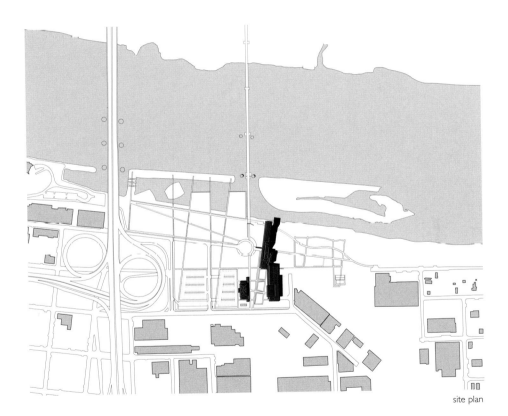

site plan

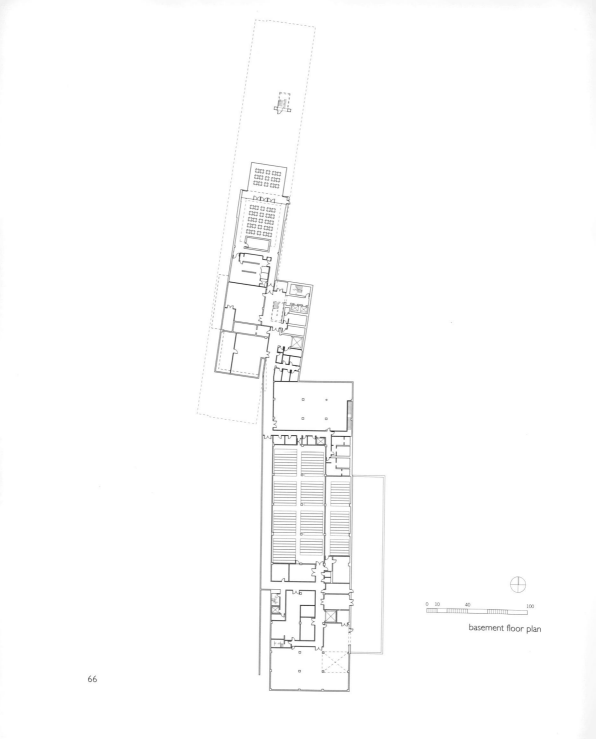

basement floor plan

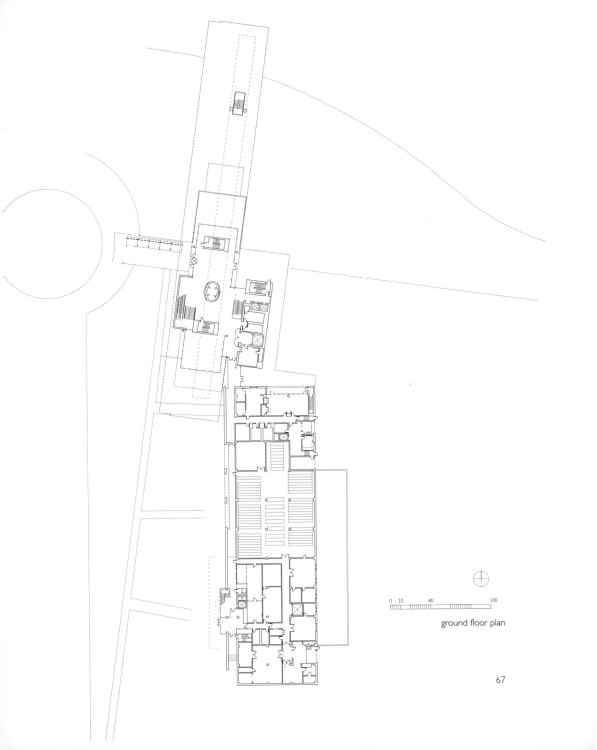

ground floor plan

0 10   40   100

67

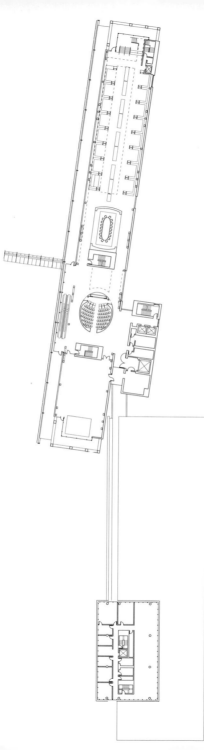

second floor plan

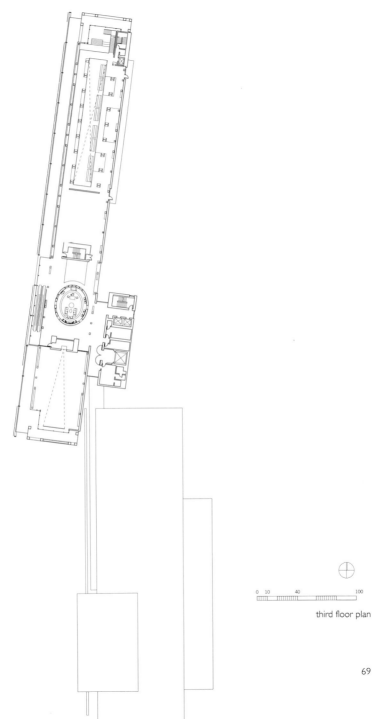

0 10   40   100

third floor plan

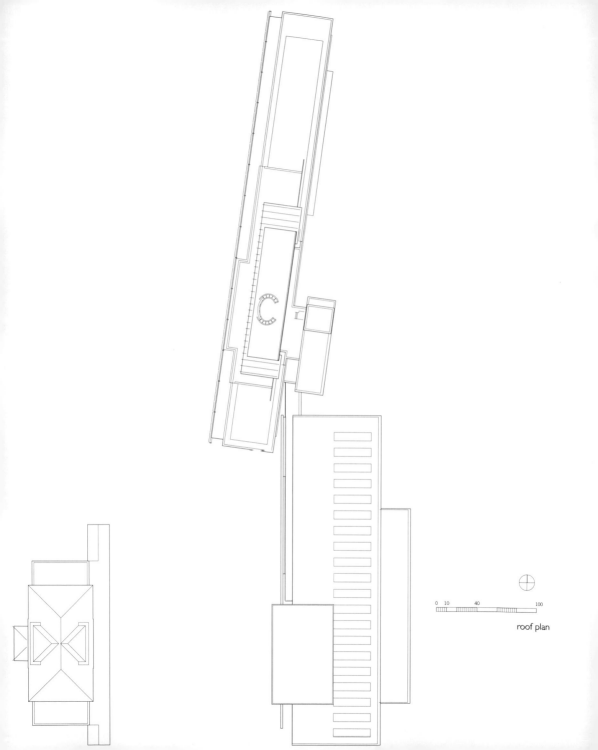

0 10   40   100

roof plan

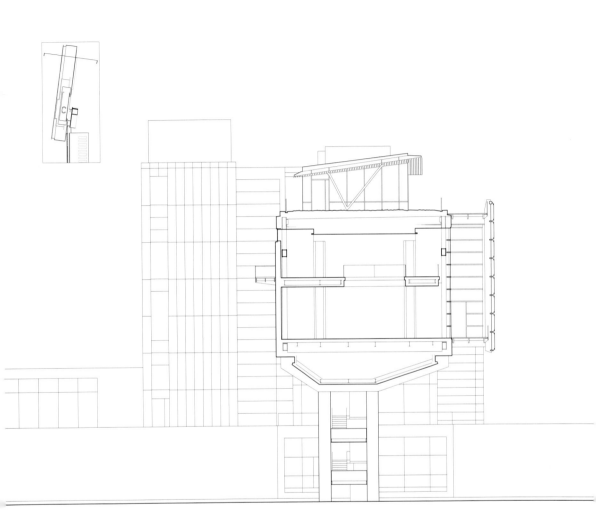

0 10   40   100

east-west section through Museum

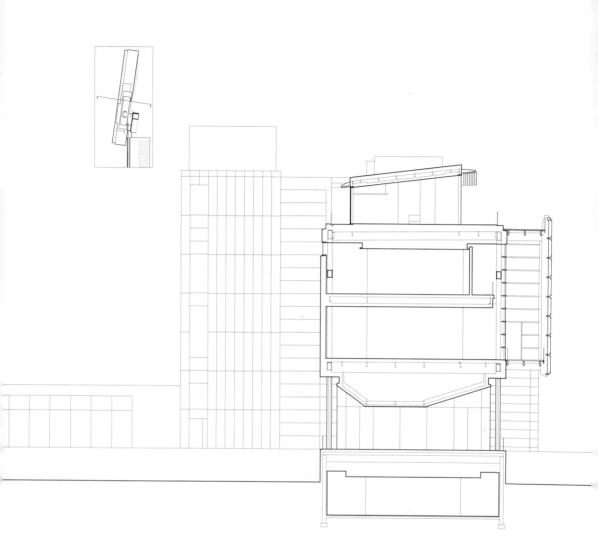

0 10   40   100

east-west section through Museum, Café and Executive Level

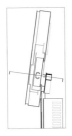

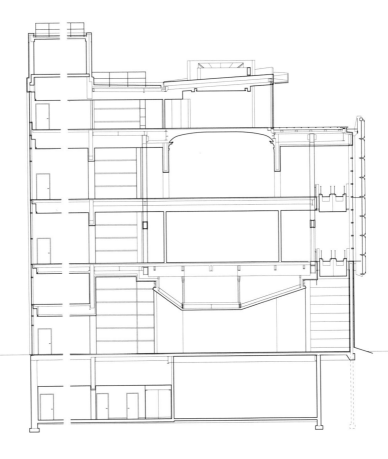

0 10   40   100

east-west section through Oval Office

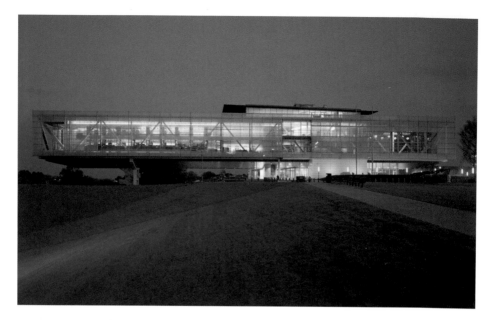

The building's west screen wall, separated from the curtain wall by an exterior walkway, acts as a sunscreen for the Museum during the day, protecting objects and substantially reducing the air conditioning required to cool the interior. Employing a special laminated glass with an integral printed interlayer of white and black dots, the screen wall is highly transparent from the interior, maximizing the view of the Park and the River beyond, while reflecting light and glare and appearing scrim-like from the exterior. Lights are filtered through a diffuser within the glass. At night, the Museum is a glowing presence, visible from downtown Little Rock and from the Interstate.

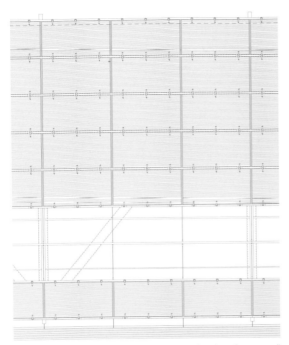

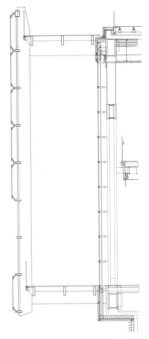

elevation of screen wall

section through exterior walkway

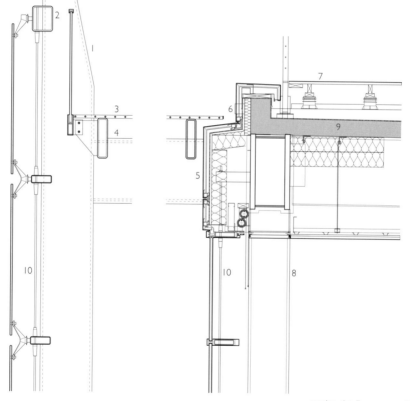

1   painted built-up steel plate vertical
2   painted steel tube horizontal
3   aluminum open grating on steel tube supports
4   built-up steel outrigger
5   aluminum composite panel
6   light fixture
7   ipe wood deck on pedestals
8   intumescent painted steel truss
9   cast-in-place concrete slab
10 stainless steel threaded dead load rod

section detail - screen wall and parapet

76

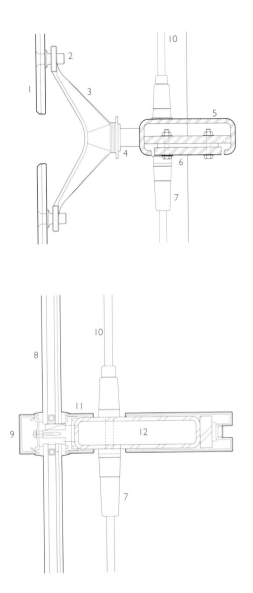

1.   low iron laminated tempered glass with printed interlayer
2.   stainless steel flush point fixing
3.   custom cast stainless steel bracket
4.   stainless steel stand off at bracket
5.   3'' × 8'' × 3/8'' painted steel tube
6.   painted steel plate connector shop-welded to vertical mullion
7.   stainless steel threaded coupler unit
8.   low iron laminated insulated glass unit with low-e coating
9.   extruded aluminum pressure plate and stainless steel clad aluminum snap cap
10.   stainless steel threaded dead load rod
11.   stainless steel clad extruded aluminum horizontal
12.   steel tube horizontal

1   painted steel plate outrigger support
2   1" x 4" ipe wood
3   threaded rod welded to bottom of plate
4   3/8" stainless steel rod
5   slotted steel plate
6   vertical adjustment nuts
7   neoprene gasket
8   flat seam zinc fascia
9   painted steel plate outrigger
10   extruded aluminum re-entrant corner mullion
11   extruded aluminum mullion
12   insulated glass door with aluminum frame
13   insulated glass with low-e coating
14   built-up steel inclined "v" column
15   steel base plates with statinless steel pin
16   ipe wood deck on pedestals

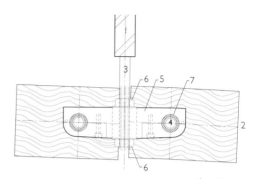

section detail

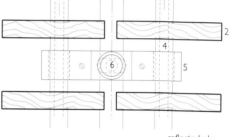

reflected plan

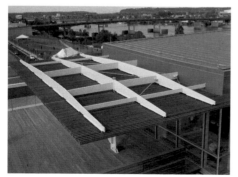

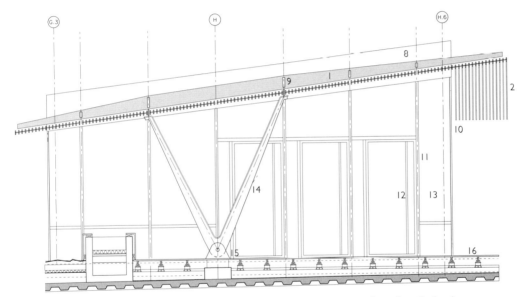

section at Executive Level sunscreen

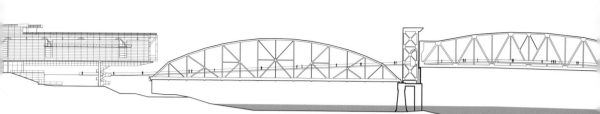

The 1899 Rock Island Railroad Bridge will be
employed as a pedestrian crossing, and will provide
a link between the Presidential Park and a future
waterfront park in North Little Rock

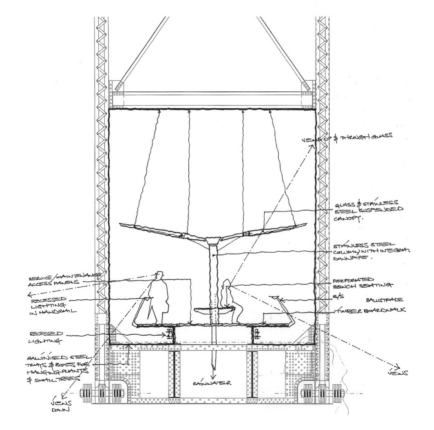

VIEWS UP & THROUGH GLASS

GLASS & STAINLESS
STEEL SUSPENDED
CANOPY.

STAINLESS STEEL
COLUMN WITH INTEGRAL
DOWNPIPE.

SERVICE/MAINTENANCE
ACCESS PANELS

PERFORATED
BENCH SEATING

S/S   BALUSTRADE

RECESSED
LIGHTING
IN HANDRAIL

TIMBER BOARDWALK

RECESSED
LIGHTING

GALVINISED STEEL
TRAYS & BOXES FOR
HANGING PLANTS
& SMALL TREES

RAINWATER

VIEWS

VIEWS
DOWN

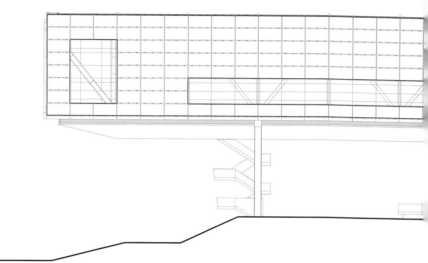

Groundbreaking   December 5, 2001
Dedication   November 18, 2004

Size: 150,000 square feet of new construction,
13,200 square feet of renovated space in
Choctaw Station.

Clinton Presidential Park: The 30-acre public
riverfront park includes active areas for festival
celebrations, theatrical and musical perform-
ances, educational use and urban fishing and
passive areas for picnicking, strolling, nature study
and bird watching. The ecological balance of the
riverbank has been restored.

Main Building: Principal public spaces include
a 20,000 square foot exhibition sequence with
orientation theater, permanent and temporary

exhibits, a multi-purpose Great Hall (220-seat
banquet or 350-seat forum), Café, Gift Shop and
classrooms. The executive apartment is located
atop the main building.

The Archive: Linked to the main building, it
contains the National Archives and Records
Administration (NARA) research and storage
facilities.

Choctaw Station: The University of Arkansas
Clinton School of Public Service, a masters
degree program, the Clinton Public Policy
Institute and the Clinton Foundation occupy
the restored historic train station.

Rock Island Railroad Bridge: The Clinton
Foundation will restore this abandoned railroad

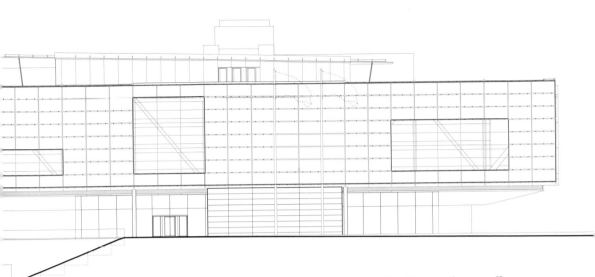

bridge as a pedestrian crossing, linking the new park and facilities to North Little Rock.

Sustainability: The Clinton Presidential Center was awarded a Silver LEED (Leadership in Energy and Environmental Design) certification from the USGBC (United States Green Building Council) in recognition of the many environmentally sustainable elements incorporated into the structure and operation of the buildings and park. Since the LEED certification initiative requires an ongoing assessment of the performance of the facility during its occupancy and use, the Clinton Presidential Center will be an active, observable laboratory for future developments in sustainable design.

CLIENT
The William J. Clinton Foundation

DESIGN TEAM
Architect: Polshek Partnership, LLP
Richard Olcott, James Polshek, Joseph Fleischer, Kevin McClurkan, Kate Mann, Molly McGowan, Megan Miller, Christen Johansen, Amy Lin, Kate Kulpa, Charmian Place, Tanya Chan, Brad Groff, Elliott Hodges, Katherine Huber, Steven Joyce, Chris Koon, Edgar Papazian, Michael Regan, Mary Rowe, Jill Sicinski, Oliver Sippl, Felicia Berger, Andrew Comfort, Oneka Home, Janny Kim, Tala Mikdashi, James Rhee, Will Rosebro, Crystal Son, David Wallance, Robert Young, Joerg Kiesow, Kwansoo Kim, Scott Melancon, Brooks Slocum

EXHIBITION DESIGN	Ralph Appelbaum Associates
PROGRAM MANAGER	Phelps Program Management, LLC
GENERAL CONTRACTOR	CDI Contractors, LLC

CONSULTANTS

Landscape Architect	Hargreaves Associates
Structural Engineer	Leslie E. Robertson Associates, RLLP
MEP Engineer	Flack + Kurtz, Inc.
Associate Architects	Polk Stanley Rowland Curzon Porter Architects, Ltd.
	Witsell Evans Rasco Architects and Planners
	Woods Carradine Architects
Associate MEP	Cromwell Architects Engineers
Associate Landscape	Landscape Architecture, Inc.
Civil/Geotechnical	McClelland Consulting Engineers
Owner's Representative	Gary Eikenhorst
Program Manager	Phelps Program Management, LLC
Specifications	Robert Schwartz & Associates
Acoustical Consultant	Cerami and Associates, Inc
Curtainwall Consultant	R. A. Heintges Architects Consultants
Signage/Graphics	Poulin + Morris Design Consultants
Lighting	Cline Bettridge Bernstein Lighting Design Inc.
Window Washing	Entek Engineering, LLP
Elevator	IROS elevator Design Services, LLC
Food Service	Next Step Design Group, Inc.
Soils Engineer	Grubbs, Hoskyn, Barton & Wyatt, Inc.
LEED Consultants	Rocky Mountain Institute, Steven Winter Associates
Security	Ducibella, Venter & Santore
ADA Consultant	LCM Architects
Fountain Consultant	Dan Euser Waterarchitecture Inc.
Irrigation Consultant	MDL Consulting
Marine Engineer	Moffatt & Nichol Engineers
Playground Design	Play.Site.Architecture